What Is
LEGO?

by Jim O'Connor

illustrated by Ted Hammond

Penguin Workshop

For my sons, Robby and Teddy, who shared LEGO
sets with me, and always wowed me with their
LEGO creations—JOC

To my kids Stephanie and Jason—TH

PENGUIN WORKSHOP
An Imprint of Penguin Random House LLC, New York

Copyright © 2020 by Penguin Random House LLC. All rights reserved.
Published by Penguin Workshop, an imprint of Penguin Random House LLC, New York.
PENGUIN and PENGUIN WORKSHOP are trademarks of Penguin Books Ltd.
WHO HQ & Design is a registered trademark of Penguin Random House LLC.
Printed in the USA.

Visit us online at www.penguinrandomhouse.com.

Library of Congress Control Number: 2019054567

ISBN 9780593092941 (paperback)   10 9 8 7 6 5 4 3 2 1
ISBN 9780593092958 (library binding)   10 9 8 7 6 5 4 3 2 1

Contents

What Is LEGO?

Billund is a very small town in Denmark, a country in northern Europe. Only about six thousand people live there. It is far away from Denmark's capital city of Copenhagen. But every year over a million and a half people visit Billund.

Why?

Because Billund is the home of the LEGO toy company. And LEGO fans from all over the world go there to visit LEGO's main factory. There, nineteen billion LEGO pieces are made every year. That's right. Nineteen billion. Those pieces come in dozens of different shapes, colors, and sizes that are used in countless different LEGO sets. Besides the original LEGO factory in Billund, there are four others, in the Czech Republic, Hungary, China, and Mexico. Altogether they make over ninety billion LEGO bricks a year. They also make seven hundred million tiny rubber tires for LEGO cars and trucks.

In Billund, the crowds of LEGO fans also visit LEGOLAND. It opened in 1968 and is a thirty-five-acre amusement park for children eleven or younger. There's the Vikings River Splash, Lloyd's Laser Maze, and roller coasters such as The Dragon, which is based on LEGO KNIGHTS KINGDOM™ sets, as well as DUPLO planes,

LEGO cars to ride, and more. But the heart of the park is Miniland, a complete miniature city made from more than twenty million LEGO bricks.

So how did the LEGO company end up in Billund? And how has LEGO grown to be the most successful toy company in the world?

The LEGO story starts in the 1930s with a very skillful carpenter who happened to live in Billund. His name was Ole Kirk Christiansen. He's among the most famous people you've never heard of!

Scandinavia

Denmark, the home of LEGO, is one of three countries known together as Scandinavia. The other two are Sweden and Norway. They are all in northern Europe. They have long, cold winters and shorter summers than most other European countries. Sweden is the largest of the three in size and population. Its capital is Stockholm. Norway has a long, rocky coastline on the parts of the North Atlantic Ocean called the North Sea and the Norwegian Sea. Its capital is Oslo. Denmark, whose capital is Copenhagen, is the smallest of the three in size. All have similar languages, although not exactly the same.

All three countries have constitutional monarchies and a parliamentary system. That means they have a king or queen who has very limited powers. The passing of laws is the job of elected members of their parliament. The head of each government is a prime minister.

Swedes, Danes, and Norwegians travel easily among the three countries. In fact, Ole Kirk Christiansen, founder of LEGO, had his first carpentry job in Norway and married a Norwegian woman. Then he returned to Denmark and set up a small business in Billund.

CHAPTER 1
A Toy Maker

Ole Kirk Christiansen was born in 1891 in a small Danish village called Filskov. He was the youngest of ten children. The Christiansens had little money. Even as a young child, Ole helped work on the family farm. For fun, he liked to carve toys for himself out of wood. As a young man, he worked for one of his older brothers and learned to become a carpenter.

Ole Kirk Christiansen

After a few years, Ole moved first to Germany

and then to Norway. He was hoping to find better work for someone with his skills. But in 1916, after Ole met and married Kirstine Sorensen, the young couple moved back to Denmark and settled in the quiet farming village of Billund.

Ole made a living fixing up old homes and building new houses. He had a shop where, besides furniture, he made handy housewares like ironing boards, stools, and ladders.

Ole and Kirstine had three sons. In 1924,

two of the boys accidentally set fire to the carpentry shop. They had been playing with wood chips. In no time, the shop burned to the ground. So did the Christiansens' house, which was right next door to the shop. All of a sudden, Ole had no home for his family and no workplace.

Ole, however, did not throw up his hands and give up. That was not his nature, even though by 1926 there was another Christiansen son to feed. He rebuilt his house as well as the shop, which ended up being bigger than the old one. Life seemed hopeful again.

But then in 1929, the world economy crashed. This was the beginning of the Great Depression that lasted through the 1930s. Millions of people in Europe and the United States lost their jobs, their savings, and even their homes.

During these years, Ole's business barely scraped by. No one could afford his ladders, furniture, or ironing boards. One by one, he had to lay off his workers. His only helper was the third of his four sons, Godtfred. Godtfred was only twelve years old.

One misfortune followed another. In 1932, Ole's wife Kirstine died. That left Ole with all the responsibility for taking care of the family. However, throughout his life Ole never let tragedies, large or small, stop him.

One bright spot even during the Depression was that people kept on buying Ole's painted wooden pull toys. Although they didn't have much money, parents still wanted their children to have fun. One of his most popular toys was a colorful wooden duck. Its beak could open and shut when it was pulled across the floor.

Sometimes, his customers didn't have enough money to pay for the toys. That was okay with Ole. He would accept farmers' vegetables and eggs as payment instead.

In time, Ole decided to forget about making practical things. Instead, he'd concentrate on turning out more colorful wooden toys. In addition to the very popular duck, he made wooden trucks and cars.

No matter how bad business was, Ole insisted that his toys had to be top quality. Once, Godtfred decided to save some money by only putting two coats of varnish on the wooden ducks instead of the usual three. When Ole heard what Godtfred had done, he was very upset. He made his son unwrap every duck and apply another coat of the varnish. Ole told Godtfred that only the best is good enough. "Only the best is good enough" became the motto of Ole's company. Godtfred carved it on a sign in the workshop for all to see.

In 1934, Ole decided to give a name to his little toy business. He based it on the Danish phrase *leg godt*, which means "play well." Ole combined the first two letters of each word to make up a name for his company . . . LEGO. It also turns out that in Latin, *lego* means "I assemble." What an amazing coincidence!

Slowly, the company began to do better. Ole was able to hire back some of the people he'd laid off. Soon LEGO was employing ten workers.

Ole began traveling around Denmark and other countries nearby to show his wooden toys to store owners. It was hard for him to talk about how good his toys were. He was not a natural salesman, but he did not give up.

In 1934, Ole was married again, to a woman named Sofie Jorgensen. Soon a new baby—a little girl called Ulla—joined the family.

Ole with his children and wife, Sofie, 1938

War waged through Europe from 1939 to 1945. Yet during this time, Ole was able to not only keep LEGO open but to expand. Things were looking up for Ole's business. Then, believe it or not, in 1942, the LEGO factory and warehouse burned down!

Did this stop Ole?

No! Once again he rebuilt, this time making the factory even bigger than before. By the next year, he was employing forty people. In time, all his sons were working for LEGO.

Ole didn't know it yet, but a revolution in the toy business was coming. And LEGO was ready for it.

CHAPTER 2
Plastic

Why was there a revolution in toy making?

It was because of one thing: plastic.

After World War II, companies began to use plastic to make toys that used to be made from wood. Plastic was cheaper than wood. It was lighter and easier to work with. It could also be made in a variety of bright colors.

The pieces for plastic toys were made using something called an injection molding machine. In 1946, LEGO bought its first one.

Here's how it worked.

Injection molding machine

Hot liquid plastic was pumped through the machine into a mold. After a very short time, the plastic cooled enough that it held the shape of the mold. Then the plastic piece was ejected from the mold and new liquid plastic could be pumped in to make more pieces.

This was a very different way of making toys. Ole's wooden toys had to be carved by hand. They took a long time to make. With machines, it was possible to make thousands of toys in just one day.

One of LEGO's first plastic toys was a small copy of a tractor made by a farm equipment company. LEGO spent more than a year designing the molds for the tractor's various parts. The designs and injection molding machine and molds cost LEGO about three times more than the price of a real tractor. But the plastic tractor was a big hit for LEGO. It could be bought already assembled. Or it could be bought in a kit that let children put together the tractor themselves.

Ole wanted to make toys that children could play with creatively. For years, LEGO had been making wooden blocks that children could stack. They were fun, to a point. But towers of blocks toppled over easily and a child couldn't really build anything very real-looking with them.

Could Ole use plastic to create something more fun?

Plastic Everywhere!

First developed in the late 1800s, plastic is a synthetic material. That means it's not found in nature. It's man-made. Plastic is used in lots of toys like LEGO, dolls, and board-game pieces. It's also used in parts of airplanes and automobiles. There are plastic cups, plates, and eating utensils. You brush your teeth with a plastic toothbrush and comb your hair with a plastic comb. There's some plastic in so many things that we use every day.

So what's so useful about plastic?

Plastic has plasticity—the ability to bend, twist, or be made into different shapes without breaking.

The reason plastic is used so widely is because it is cheap and can replace other materials such as wood, glass, or metal.

The first injection molding machine that Ole bought happened to come with some little plastic building bricks. They were samples to show what the machine could do. Called Self-Locking Building Bricks, they had been made by a British company called Kiddicraft. Little studs on the top of each brick could fit into the hollow bottom of another brick. Once connected, the bricks held together.

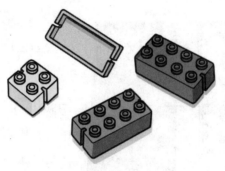

Kiddicraft bricks

Ole and Godtfred were impressed with these self-locking bricks. They could be put together in all kinds of ways. So Ole tried making some plastic bricks that were similar to Kiddicraft's but ones that he thought were designed better. They had squared-off corners and flattened tops on the studs.

Unfortunately, these first LEGO bricks did not work as well as Ole and Godtfred had hoped. They cracked. They didn't fit together snugly enough. If Ole's bricks didn't snap together perfectly—and unsnap easily—building with them would be no fun. And, of course, the bricks would be of no use if they broke.

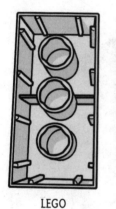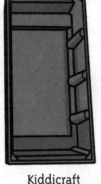

LEGO   Kiddicraft

So new bricks were designed. The inside of each brick had hollow tubes that the studs on another brick could grasp much more firmly. New molds were made and out came new little plastic bricks. Ole was so confident about the new type of brick that he got a patent for it.

What Is a Patent?

When a person comes up with a new invention like a lightbulb (Thomas Edison), a computer system (Steve Jobs), or a toy (Ole Christiansen), they don't want others to copy it and make money from something they created.

A patent is a document given to an inventor that protects the inventor from copycats. To get one, the inventor must present a detailed description of the product, including drawings and sometimes models, to the patent office in their country.

Usually, a patent lasts for twenty years.

Were they an immediate success?

No!

In 1951, Ole became sick. He was now sixty years old. He knew that the company needed a younger man to run it. He chose Godtfred. After all, Godtfred had worked alongside his father since childhood. He had designed many of LEGO's first products.

Although Godtfred was head of the company, Ole stayed involved throughout the early 1950s. He insisted that an even larger factory be built. And he watched over the final design changes that were made to LEGO bricks.

Amazingly, the basic brick (called the 2x4) has not changed since then. The LEGO bricks that are made now will fit with bricks from 1958!

Ole passed away in 1958 just as the new improved bricks were introduced. From 1958 through 1960, LEGO sent free sample boxes to toy stores to show how well the bricks fit together.

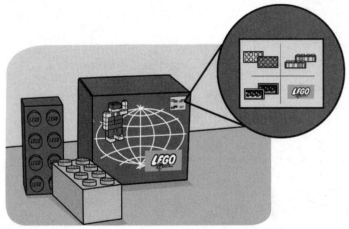

They contained only two bricks. Today, those original little LEGO boxes are collectors' items.

And then in 1960, disaster struck once more. You may find it hard to believe, but there was yet another fire! The factory didn't burn down this time, but all the plans and drawings for the old wooden toys were destroyed. An important part of LEGO's early history was lost.

After this, Godtfred decided that it was time to completely stop making wooden toys. The company would only make plastic LEGO bricks.

CHAPTER 3
LEGO Takes Off!

Sometimes complaints are really helpful to hear.

While Godtfred was at a toy show in England, a buyer complained to him that LEGOs should have a "system."

What did he mean by that?

Along with a kit of bricks that could build one house, there should be other kits of bricks for other kinds of buildings. And all the kits should be played with together.

Godtfred knew the toy buyer was right.

When he got back to Billund, he told the designers to find some way for different LEGO kits to interact. They came up with an idea called the LEGO Town Plan. It had a gray plastic base with sections of studs to fit houses on.

LEGO started to produce sets for all the different buildings in LEGO Town. From the start, little plastic trees and bushes were also made to put in the Town's parks and yards.

Kids loved the LEGO Town system. It came with bricks in two different sizes—the 2x4 and the smaller 2x2. Kids started building their own houses using their imagination. They were able to do this because the bricks in different sets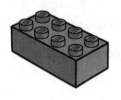

2x4 brick   2x2 brick

could all fit together. This truly was what LEGO was all about—playing well.

In 1962, Godtfred Christiansen spelled out the qualities that every LEGO system should have. They were all qualities that his father Ole would have approved of:

1. Unlimited play potential—which meant you weren't done with it ever. You could always find new things to make out of the bricks.

2. Fun for boys and girls

3. Fun for every age—this certainly is

true, as there are so many grown-ups who love building with LEGO

4. Year-round play
5. Healthy, quiet play
6. Long hours of play
7. Development of imagination and creativity
8. The more LEGO, the greater the value
9. Extra sets always available
10. Quality in every detail

On the box of the first LEGO Town system there was a drawing of a house that could be assembled from the bricks included in the box. However, there weren't any instructions on how to build that house.

That changed in 1964. LEGO began including a leaflet with instructions.

Reading detailed instructions can often be a very frustrating experience. So LEGO did something new. They left out all the words. They used pictures—only pictures—instead.

The instructions consisted of step-by-step pictures of a project from start to finish. Each step was easy to follow. It showed which size brick to use and how many. Every picture showed the model from an angle with the new bricks added on.

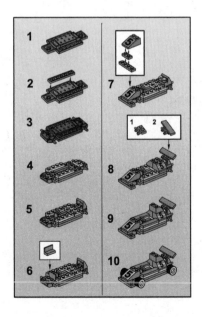

LEGO still doesn't use written instructions. Children don't need to read to follow them. Almost anyone can follow the building process from the numbered pictures and figure out where the bricks belong.

This was a great decision. Although sets were becoming bigger and more complicated, the instructions made building them easy.

CHAPTER 4
How Are LEGO Bricks Made?

All LEGO bricks are made the exact same way. They begin as tiny plastic grains in different colors. Truckloads are brought to a LEGO factory where they are stored in huge towers called silos. (Farms have tall silos, too—for storing grain.)

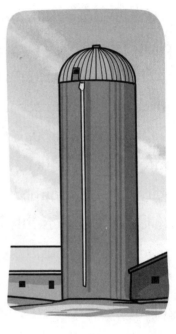

Silo

Originally there were five colors—red, yellow, blue, white, and green. Today there are over sixty different colors.

The plastic grains are fed into pipes and sent to the correct injection molding machine for the color, size, and shape that are needed at that particular time. The grains are melted at very hot temperatures (about 450 degrees Fahrenheit) and mixed together until they turn into a thick plastic soup.

The liquid plastic is poured into metal molds. After only fifteen seconds, the plastic hardens. It is already cool enough for the bricks to be spit out onto a conveyor belt. At the end of the conveyor belt, they are dumped into large crates.

Once a crate is filled with the correct number of identical bricks, it is marked with a bar code. (A bar code tells the size, shape, and color of the bricks in a particular crate.) A robot forklift comes and takes the crate directly to a warehouse where the crate is stacked with other crates with the same bar code.

When the different bricks in a set are needed,

the robots return to the warehouse, find the correct crates, and take them to the assembly department. Each size, shape, and color brick is loaded into a machine that puts the correct number of them into a bin. Each bin is weighed to make sure it has the right number of bricks in it. The bin travels by conveyor belt to another machine, which seals the correct number of bricks in small, clear plastic bags.

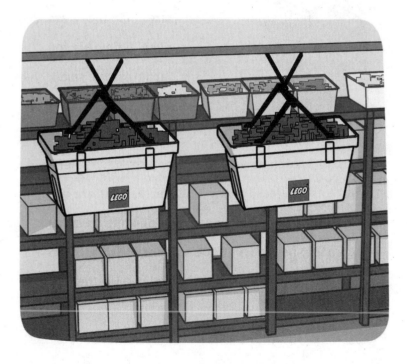

Quality Control

When bricks are being made, sample ones are randomly selected and sent to the quality control department. There they are inspected, measured,  and weighed to be sure the bricks are exactly the right size. If they are even a tiny bit too large or too small, they won't have what LEGO calls the correct "clutch power." They won't snap together—and unsnap—easily. Any LEGO bricks that are not perfect are sent back and melted down to be made again into new bricks. LEGO says that only eighteen out of every one million bricks fail the quality control test!

All the different bags of bricks needed for a set are sent down chutes into the familiar LEGO boxes with a photo of the completed set on the cover. LEGO employees double-check that each box contains all the bags needed. The instructions are put in. Then the top goes on the box and it is sealed.

Finally, the LEGO sets are put into larger cartons and shipped to toy stores around the world.

When you're in a toy store, you'll notice that the box for every LEGO set states what age it's for. The first ones were intended for children older than five. The company thought that younger children would have a hard time snapping the bricks together and taking them apart. The company also worried that small children might put the bricks into their mouths and possibly choke. However, LEGO heard that younger children *were* playing with the bricks.

So in 1969, LEGO started bringing out DUPLO sets. The DUPLO plastic bricks were exactly twice the size of standard LEGO bricks. They were designed for younger children with smaller hands. Because of their size, they were safe for children as young as one and a half years old.

The company made DUPLO versions of the best-selling LEGO sets like the farm and police station.

DUPLO took a while to catch on. The company advertised that as children grew older, they could still use DUPLO bricks with LEGO bricks. They fit together perfectly.

While DUPLO is for toddlers, the most complicated LEGO sets are marked for ages twelve and up. That includes grown-ups of all ages who have never grown tired of playing with LEGO!

CHAPTER 5
Branching Out

The LEGO Town system was followed by others, all on themes popular with young children—pirate sets, farm sets, and castles. In fact, LEGO has introduced more than two hundred castle-themed sets, including a Japanese Flying Ninja's Fortress.

The Flying Ninja's Fortress came out in 1998.

It is a great example of how much thought is put into every LEGO toy set. The Fortress can be assembled in three ways. It loosely copies the style of fortresses in Japan from centuries past when warriors—ninjas (foot soldiers) and samurais (knights)—fought to protect a lord's land.

There are nine minifigures. Seven are warriors who come with armor, helmets, and weapons. A flying contraption with moveable wings can be attached to the minifigures. In addition, there is a trapdoor and a treasure chest (with tiny treasure inside), and even a jail for the robber minifigure.

NINJAGO

In 2011, LEGO came out with a system for an imaginary world called NINJAGO. NINJAGO was based on a mix of Japanese and Chinese myths. The sets in this system became enormously popular. In addition to the fun of construction, there were biographies for each Ninja minifigure. This inspired kids to role-play (in role-play, kids imagine they are the different characters and act out different adventures with them).

The success of NINJAGO and the animated TV series on Cartoon Network led to a full-length movie that came out in 2017.

Other popular castles made by LEGO include Sleeping Beauty's Castle from Disney's amusement parks (it's one of the largest sets LEGO makes). There is also Princess Elsa's castle from the *Frozen* movies. LEGO is allowed to make these toy sets because it has signed an agreement with Disney. For every Elsa's castle that is sold, LEGO pays Disney some money. This is called having a license. Over time, LEGO has had many licenses, for example, *The Simpsons*, *Pirates of the Caribbean*, and its most popular licensed line of all: *Star Wars*.

Way back in 1978, LEGO introduced the Space system, reflecting children's fascination with the great beyond. There were rocket ships, a space station, and so on. But there was no story line connecting the different sets.

One year earlier, 1977, *Star Wars* had played in movie theaters all across the United States. It was the first of nine megahit films. And its story line seemed to fit perfectly for LEGO toys.

It is now more than twenty years

since LEGO first made a deal with Lucasfilm. (George Lucas is the creator of *Star Wars*.) It has produced LEGO sets for all the *Star Wars* movies. Some of the most intricate and impressive LEGO sets

copy things seen in the films, such as the Death Star, the cantina in the first movie, and the *Millennium Falcon*.

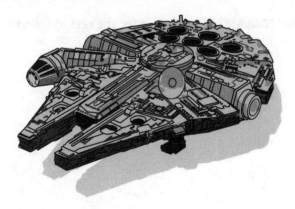

The Biggest LEGO Vehicle Ever Built

On May 23, 2013, a forty-three-foot-long X-Wing Starfighter appeared in New York City's Times Square. It was built out of 5,334,200 LEGO bricks and weighed almost 46,000 pounds. It took thirty-two LEGO master builders about four months to build it in the LEGO model shop in the Czech Republic. Then it traveled to the United States inside a freight ship and was moved to Times Square. It stayed there for three days before it was moved to the LEGOLAND in California for the rest of the year.

CHAPTER 6
LEGO's Little People

The only things missing from the first LEGO systems were "people" to inhabit the houses and buildings. And that didn't last for long.

The first little "people"—a family of four—came out in 1974. A year later, police officer

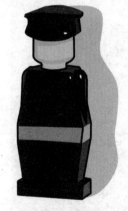

figures were added. Their uniform was painted on them. Each of the four police officers was in a different pose. But their arms and legs didn't move and they didn't have faces.

Little LEGO police 1975

Over time, LEGO improved their minifigures—that's what the company called them.

First came arms that moved. These minifigures were known as stiffys. Then later minifigures came with legs that moved, too.

1978 LEGO police   1978 LEGO doctor

Today, the standard LEGO minifigure has nine parts: head, body, hip joint, two arms, two hands for gripping things, and two legs. At least eight thousand different minifigures have been created for the various LEGO toy sets. Most LEGO sets come with a certain number of minifigures. Space station sets, for example, include astronauts. Bags of minifigures are also sold separately.

Playmobil

Playmobil toy sets were introduced in the 1970s by a German toy company. The Playmobil sets do not use bricks. Instead, they have plastic pieces— like the walls and roof of a castle—that snap together. They also have small plastic figures that go with the theme of the playset. For example, knights for a castle.

Playmobil started coming out with plastic people before LEGO did. The Playmobil toys appeal to about the same age group as young LEGO builders and are on many of the same themes. Playmobil toys are popular, but not nearly as popular as LEGO. They do not offer the possibility of combining pieces or designing entirely new structures.

The majority of minifigures have black eyes. Nonhuman ones, such as monsters, have colored eyes. Child minifigures have larger eyes than the grown-ups and often have freckles. Among all the minifigures, there are over six hundred different facial expressions. Sometimes a minifigure has more than one expression! For example, if a minifigure has a sad or upset face, there may be a happy face printed on the back of the head. A child can just turn the head around, adjust the wig or hat, and suddenly the minifigure is all smiles.

Probably what strikes anyone first is the color of the head on minifigures. Nearly all have bright yellow heads. Bright yellow was chosen because no real people have skin that color. At LEGO.com, the company explains that they felt this was a way for no child to feel left out.

Some minifigures do have other color "skin"— e.g., brown, pale pinkish-white. But the website says those figures "are usually based on characters we didn't create," such as ones in movies that LEGO has based toys on.

The vast majority of LEGO minifigures are male. There are way fewer female minifigures. There have been some complaints about this. Perhaps there's such a difference because it's estimated that boys—real ones!—make up about 90 percent of LEGO's audience.

As for its female minifigures, LEGO has sometimes been criticized for sticking to stereotypes. It wasn't until 1993 that the first female astronaut was included in a Space set. In real life, the first female American astronaut—Sally Ride— flew into space ten years earlier in 1983.

Sally Ride

Also causing some controversy were the LEGO Friends sets. They were first introduced in 2012. LEGO purposely designed them to appeal to girls. The *i* in the word *Friends* is dotted with a heart; the different sets include lots of hot-pink bricks, which are used for building a hair salon, a dressing room, and a supermarket, among other things. Critics thought that these sets reinforced out-of-date ideas about what girls were like or wanted to become.

LEGO Friends sets, however, were a huge hit.

Girls loved them. LEGO made lots of money while also getting more customers for their toys. (Remember, one of Godtfred's hopes was that LEGO would be toys for boys and girls.) And some parents were glad to see more girls building and constructing with LEGO Friends. That was important to them.

What do you think? Take a look at a Friends set—maybe you or a friend already own one—and decide for yourself.

CHAPTER 7
Good Times/Tough Times

In 1973, Godtfred Kirk Christiansen stepped down as managing director of the company. Someone else ran it until 1979. After that, Godtfred's son Kjeld Kirk Kristiansen replaced him. (In Denmark, the name Christiansen can be spelled with either a C or a K.)

LEGO was thriving. Godtfred had opened plants in Germany,

Kjeld Kirk Kristiansen

Great Britain, and the United States. New sets were being introduced all the time.

In 1977, LEGO brought out the Expert Builder sets. Kids could make more complicated constructions such as tractors, forklifts, and even a helicopter.

LEGO Expert Builder helicopter

Then in 1986, the LEGO Technic sets replaced the Expert Builder sets. Technic was a big advance from Expert Builders. Technic sets were designed for older LEGO users, aged seven to fourteen. There were racing cars, motorcycles, trucks, airplanes, helicopters, and different farm equipment such as tractors. They used batteries to power motors and compressed air pumps. The motors turned wheels that moved cars and trucks and gears that worked with pulleys to lift loads. Instead of studs on bricks, beams and pins were used for construction.

LEGO Technic street motorcycle

Although tiny, the vehicles and equipment looked very realistic.

The designers working on Technic followed three rules: The small vehicle or piece of equipment in each kit had to resemble quite closely a full-sized one. Each Technic kit made something that copied at least one function (action) of the real equipment or vehicle. And every kit encouraged builders to learn new techniques and to devise their own version of what was being constructed.

Kjeld continued to make the company grow bigger and bigger. But by the late 1980s, a whole new kind of entertainment was pulling young people away from LEGO.

Video games.

They were loud and colorful, with characters whose actions the players controlled. They were exciting to play and set up for head-to-head competition between players. When a game was over, all a player had to do was push a button and start again.

When LEGO saw what was happening, it decided to launch its own video games. They failed. Most of LEGO's video games just weren't as good as what kids were used to playing. The video game industry was very tough, aggressive, and fast-moving, and it needed talented young programmers who created the fantasy worlds kids wanted. LEGO didn't have the right mind-set to be a video game company. "Healthy, quiet play" was what the company had believed in.

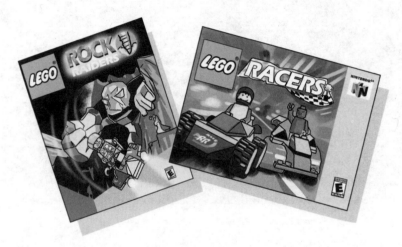

LEGO video games

In 2003, LEGO had its worst year in its history. For the first time, their sales were down and the company lost money.

Was there a future for LEGO?

CHAPTER 8
A New Leader

Kjeld knew that to survive, LEGO needed to identify the company's problems and fix them quickly. LEGO hired a young man named Jorgen Vig Knudstorp to study the company's business and come up with some ideas.

Jorgen Vig Knudstorp

Jorgen came up with a plan that Kjeld liked very much . . . Not only did he like the plan, he felt sure that Jorgen was the man to make it work. So Kjeld resigned as president in 2004. He put Jorgen (known as JVK to everyone at LEGO) in his place. For the first time in its history, LEGO was going to be led by someone who wasn't in the Christiansen family.

It turned out to be a great decision.

Jorgen decided that LEGO needed to "focus on the brick" rather than expanding into new types of entertainment such as video games or theme parks.

The LEGOLAND amusement parks were not profitable. So LEGO sold them to a company that had experience running amusements parks. (LEGO kept a small part of the ownership.) They stopped making sets that didn't sell well. And Jorgen went back to the company's greatest strength—innovation—the ability to do things in a new way.

Jorgen's Special Business Card

Front   Back

Instead of just a regular white business card, Jorgen had something special made up. It was a 3-D minifigure that looked like him. His email address and phone number were stamped on the back. What a cool thing to do!

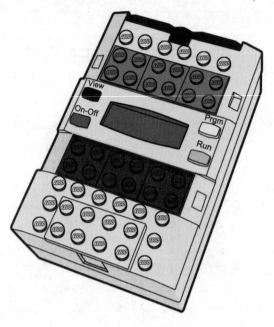

LEGO "intelligent" brick

LEGO had already introduced an "intelligent" brick that could be programmed in the late 1990s. For instance, it could control certain movements of a LEGO robot. But now LEGO made these intelligent invention sets (which are called MINDSTORMS) with more powerful programing and, at the same time, made them easier to use.

A True Story

In 2014, a twelve-year-old boy named Shubham Banerjee used MINDSTORMS EV3 to invent a lightweight, quiet, and inexpensive braille printer. Braille is a

system of raised dots on paper that allows people with visual impairments to read. A person reads braille by running their fingertips over the dots that form words and sentences.

Shubham named his printer Braigo, which is a combination of *braille* and *LEGO*. It cost around $350, where others being sold cost over $2,000. The Intel computer company was so impressed that it has invested in Shubham's invention.

In 2009, LEGO released MINDSTORMS NXT 2.0, which even had touch sensors and light sensors. After that, LEGO devised a program that gave builders complete control over their LEGO robots, using their smartphone or computer. The LEGO intelligent bricks kept getting smarter and smarter!

LEGO BIONICLEs

Another new LEGO series, BIONICLE, built a strong fan base and became immensely popular in the early 2000s. These action figures were aimed at boys eight and older. The BIONICLEs had a very cool feature: ball and socket joints that let the figures move in ways that weren't possible before.

Also, for the first time, an original story, appearing on LEGO's website, told of the warring BIONICLEs and their imaginary world. The Toa, usually good characters, fought against the evil Makuta. Originally, BIONICLE was going to be sold for just a year. But the theme was such a hit that new sets came out for years. The BIONICLE team began getting emails from kids with suggestions for improving the BIONICLE story lines and characters. LEGO used some of the kids' ideas and that made BIONICLEs grow even more popular.

LEGO also brought out new BIONICLE characters much more quickly and added new story lines every six months. Animated CDs, then videos, kept fans up to date on the plot. In time, LEGO also put out BIONICLE comic books and novels, and created a Netflix series.

But BIONICLE aroused some anger. There were complaints from Maori people, a native people who live in New Zealand. The names of some BIONICLE characters came from words in the Maori language, and they found this disrespectful. So LEGO agreed to change the names of certain characters. This switch was built into the BIONICLE story. Characters received their new name in a ceremony celebrating their bravery or honor.

As for BIONICLE, it became known as the toy that saved LEGO from going out of business.

CHAPTER 9
Designing LEGO Sets

By far the most important place at the LEGO headquarters in Billund is the Creative Campus. It's a top secret building where new LEGO systems are created. Teams of LEGO designers work on every part of a new set.

LEGO headquarters currently under construction in Billund

If it's a rocket ship, how big will it be? What is its purpose? Does it need weapons? Will it have some new feature never seen before?

A team of designers will create many different models, sometimes as many as forty, until they decide on the best one. The job of a designer is key to LEGO's success: It's the dream of so many fans all over the world to become one.

There are people who have been hoping for this career since they were small children. Some apply to the company as soon as they finish school. Some work in a business for a few years and then decide to take a chance at landing a job at LEGO.

All must have a talent for building as well as a passion for LEGO. First they must send in pictures or actual samples of their own designs. They are interviewed over Skype.

After that, every year between twenty and forty candidates are invited to go to Billund for more interviews and tests. Well before the candidates arrive at headquarters, they are sent a bag with LEGO pieces. They are told to design a new LEGO world using them.

Later in Billund, their models are reviewed by some of LEGO's senior designers. If their models are good enough, candidates are divided into small groups. A huge pile of all shapes and sizes of LEGO is poured in front of them. Each person starts building something new on the spur of the moment. When they finish, they are judged again.

Because minifigures are an important part of LEGO sets, job candidates also must draw a design for a new LEGO minifigure.

Besides having a great deal of talent, candidates must be the right "fit" for LEGO. They need to like being part of a team where everyone works together.

Finalists get to spend more time with senior designers and then have a final build, where, yet again, they must create a new LEGO set. They present their work to the top designers and explain what it is and how it works.

Then all the hopefuls go home—to places all over the world. There they wait to hear if they will be offered a job. If lucky enough to be chosen, they will move to Billund and become part of the LEGO family—made up of about two hundred designers.

A new hire starts off as an apprentice, learning from more experienced designers called senior builders. Among senior builders, the best are promoted to the title of master builder.

The odds of landing a job as a designer are terribly small. That doesn't stop lots of people from spending a significant part of their life on LEGO. They are called AFOLs (Adult Friends of LEGO) and are dedicated superfans.

Bright Ideas

A company-run website named LEGO IDEAS lets fans comment on things that are still in development and submit their own ideas for LEGO sets. If an idea gets ten thousand "yes" votes from fans, the company gives it serious consideration. A team of LEGO designers and executives pick some to actually put into production. The LEGO fan who came up with the idea is named an official LEGO designer and earns royalties. That means the creator will get a certain amount of money for every set sold.

Usually, they're people who've been playing with LEGO for as long as they can remember. As they get older, AFOLs just become more and more dedicated (or maybe the right word is obsessed).

A LEGO convention called BrickCon, 2017

Some AFOLs try to collect and build every LEGO set there is. They search for rare LEGO sets to own. They follow websites about LEGO, watch—or create—videos on YouTube, and meet other fans at LEGO conventions.

Sometimes AFOLs create their own websites or publish their own LEGO magazines.

Many AFOLs build special sets of their own invention. These are called MOCs for My Own Creations. One man made very accurate LEGO sculptures of over seventy different varieties of birds. Three of them—a hummingbird, a robin, and a blue jay—were accepted by LEGO and sold in official LEGO sets called Birds.

One of the most famous MOCs is just called *Yellow*. It's a larger-than-life sculpture of a man from the waist up, made completely of yellow bricks. He has torn his chest open and more yellow bricks pour out onto the table in front of him.

The Big Five

What are the largest LEGO sets? Which have the most pieces or take up the most space? The answers change from year to year as new sets become available.

Here are the current top five:

1. *Millennium Falcon* from Star Wars has 7,541 pieces.

2. Hogwarts Castle from the Harry Potter series has 6,020 pieces and comes with twenty-seven microfigures and four minifigures. Besides the castle, the set includes Hagrid's Hut and the Whomping Willow.

3. The Taj Mahal, a model of a famous tomb in India, has 5,923 pieces.

4. Ultimate Collector's *Millennium Falcon* had 5,197 pieces but is no longer sold.

5. NINJAGO City has 4,867 pieces with three separate levels.

Taj Mahal

Some MOCs are so large, they need a team of AFOLs to build them. In 2015, a 114-foot-tall tower was built by children to raise money for a charity. The tower was as tall as an eleven-story building! It took five days to complete and used more than half a million LEGO bricks.

There are literally thousands of MOCs online now. Videos of AFOLs constructing MOCs are fun to watch. They show how building problems are solved and how a design can change and grow.

All it takes to make an MOC is some time to sit down with a pile of random LEGO bricks and start putting them together. You don't need to have any plan. Who knows what fantastic new MOC you'll create!

Help, I Lost a LEGO Brick!

Uh-oh! A brick in a new set has gone missing. Don't despair. First, see if one of your friends has an extra of the brick you need. Second, go to the LEGO.com website. Scroll down to the bottom and, under "Customer Service," click "Replacement Parts." Follow the directions for purchasing what you need. There are also companies that sell individual LEGO bricks. Check out Toypro.com or Brickowl.com.

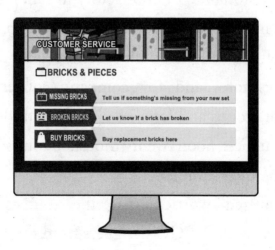

CHAPTER 10
LEGO around the World

It is safe to say that Ole Kirk Christiansen could never have imagined the impact his little plastic bricks would have on the world. Or that the company itself would be of such interest to people.

During Godtfred's time, more and more fans began visiting the LEGO factory in Billund. One of the main attractions was the model shop. Every year LEGO designers built cool models for display in toy stores and toy company conventions. School groups and families visited Billund to see these models. Soon twenty thousand tourists were coming each summer.

Godtfred worried that the tourists were distracting the LEGO designers from their work.

His solution was to move the models out of the shop and create a complete outdoor Miniland. He was inspired by a miniature city in the Netherlands (a country not far from Denmark) that had been popular since its opening in 1952.

A team of LEGO designers and model makers began building models of real Danish homes, stores, train stations, and roadways. They were built to be one-twentieth the size of the real structures. The original Miniland opened on June 7, 1968.

There were 3,000 visitors the first day and 625,000 the first year. Suddenly, tiny Billund was a tourist attraction.

Besides Miniland, an amusement park was added. Although the company now has only part ownership in the parks, there are LEGOLANDs in seven countries. There are two in the United States. One is in Florida and the other is in California, which had the first LEGOLAND water park. A third is set to open in New York State sometime in 2020.

LEGOLANDs have many different areas, each with rides and activities tied to a theme. For example, Knights' Kingdom in Denmark has a King's Castle action and stunt show.

In NINJAGO World, kids use their Ninja skills to climb rock walls or sneak through a Lloyd's Laser Maze. DUPLO Land is for the youngest children. It has a train ride where the engine and cars look as if they were built from DUPLO Bricks.

An over six-hundred-seat theater shows LEGO movies, complete with special effects like wind, water, and even aromas that go with the movie's plot.

LEGOLANDs also have LEGO-themed hotels, such as the LEGO Castle Hotel. Visitors can be surrounded by LEGO twenty-four hours a day! Maybe that seems like a little too much, but for millions of people every year, it is their idea of a perfect vacation.

For them, there is no better toy in the world and no better way to spend their free time.

There are also indoor playgrounds called LEGOLAND Discovery Centers geared for children three to ten years old. They have some rides and a Miniland. They also have LEGO master builders on hand to show kids cool tricks and shortcuts in construction. Also, a LEGO building area has lots and lots of loose bricks for kids to practice and play with.

LEGOLAND Discovery Center

In North America alone there are Discovery Centers in eleven states in the United States and one in Canada.

Then in 2014, LEGO minifigures became movie stars! *The LEGO Movie* was an animated action-adventure film. It made $469 million across the world. That's huge! It was produced by Warner Bros. Entertainment Inc. under a licensing agreement with LEGO. A second movie came out in 2019. It was called *The LEGO Movie 2: The Second Part.* It had the same cast of LEGO minifigures and a plot that echoed the first movie.

The company that Ole started in his carpentry shop nearly a century ago continues to grow, change, and win new fans. No matter where they live on the planet, kids can use LEGO sets to widen their imagination, discover new skills, and lose themselves in hours of fun. Ole Christiansen would be happy to know how many millions of children are "playing well."

Problems with Plastic

There are two big problems with plastic. First, making it uses processes that are harmful to the environment. Second, when people are done using a plastic product, they discard it. It is not biodegradable. It does not decompose or rot away. It just stays around taking up space.

One way to eliminate all that waste is to recycle plastic. Recycled soda bottles, for instance, can be made into a kind of fleece.

Another approach is to find a way to make biodegradable plastic. LEGO is experimenting with a biodegradable plastic made from sugarcane. Bioplastics can also be made from other natural materials such as starch.

Unfortunately, so far none of the bioplastics are as strong as traditional plastic. LEGO uses a huge amount of plastic every year. It has promised to switch to something that is more eco-friendly for 100 percent of its toys by 2030.

Timeline of LEGO

1891 — Ole Kirk Christiansen is born in Filskov, Denmark

1916 — Ole and his wife, Kirstine, move from Norway back to Denmark

1924 — Ole's carpentry shop burns down but is quickly rebuilt

1932 — Kirstine dies, leaving Ole with four sons

1934 — Ole names his toy company LEGO

1942 — The LEGO factory and warehouse burn down

1949 — LEGO begins manufacturing plastic bricks for building

1955 — LEGO introduces its first "system of play"—a town

— LEGO bricks are redesigned to snap and unsnap easily

1958 — Ole dies and his son Godtfred becomes president of LEGO

1969 — DUPLO sets first appear

1978 — The first LEGO minifigures come out

1979 — Godtfred's son Kjeld takes over

2003 — LEGO has its worst year in its history

2004 — Kjeld retires and names Jorgen Vig Knudstorp, a non-family member, as head of LEGO

2014 — *The LEGO Movie* opens and is a huge hit

2019 — *The LEGO Movie 2: The Second Part* opens but is not as popular as the first movie

Timeline of the World

1897	Thomas Edison patents his movie camera, called the Kinetograph
1914	World War I breaks out in Europe and lasts four years
1928	Disney's *Steamboat Willie*, introducing Mickey Mouse, is released
1929	The Great Depression begins
1932	Amelia Earhart becomes the first woman to fly solo across the Atlantic Ocean
1936	Nazi dictator Adolf Hitler opens the Summer Olympic Games in Berlin
1969	The US astronaut Neil Armstrong becomes the first human to step foot on the moon
1974	The Playmobil line of playsets and plastic figures is introduced
1977	The movie *Star Wars* opens
1979	Sony unveils the Walkman, the first personal music device to play cassettes
1985	NES, Nintendo's first game consoles, are sold
1994	Nelson Mandela becomes the first black president of South Africa
2005	Hurricane Katrina strikes the US Gulf Coast in August
2016	Donald Trump is elected president of the United States

Bibliography

*Books for young readers

**Absolutely Everything You Need to Know: Stacks of LEGO Facts*. New York: DK Publishing, 2017.

Herman, Sarah. *A Million Little Bricks: The Unofficial Illustrated History of the LEGO Phenomenon*. New York: Skyhorse Publishing, 2012.

"Inside the World of Lego." YouTube video, 1:12:36, originally aired on National Geographic Documentaries, December 20, 2015, posted by Evie Funk, December 10, 2017, https://www.youtube.com/watch?v=jm5ir5QojII.

Robertson, David C. *Brick by Brick: How LEGO Rewrote the Rules of Innovation and Conquered the Global Toy Industry*. With Bill Breen. New York: Crown Business, 2013.

*Slater, Lee. *LEGO Manufacturers: The Kristiansen Family*. Minneapolis: Abdo Publishing, 2016.

Websites

Brothers-Brick.com

LEGO.com

Toysnbricksforum.com

LEGOLAND in Billund, Denmark

An early wooden toy train manufactured by LEGO

Godtfred Kirk Christiansen, the second president of LEGO

Children play with LEGO DUPLO bricks, 1981.

The reception area at the LEGO headquarters in Billund, Denmark

A LEGO factory worker inspects bricks.

Jorgen Vig Knudstorp was the first non-family member
to run the LEGO company.

LEGO woman minifigures

Replica of an X-Wing Starfighter at LEGOLAND California, 2013

Guests attend a LEGO convention in Helsinki, Finland, in 2019.

LEGO NINJAGO toy with minifigures

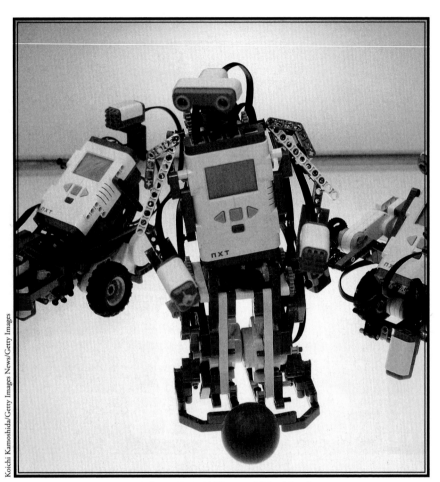

LEGO MINDSTORMS NXT robot

LEGO Friends set

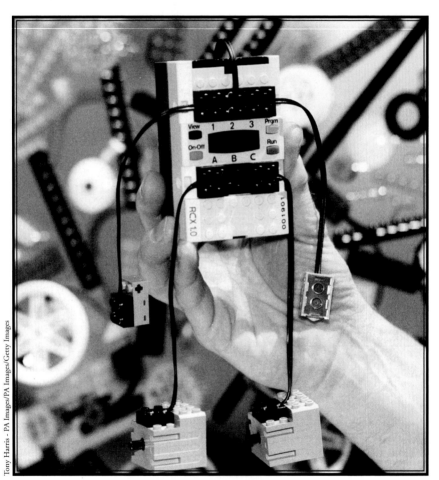

LEGO "intelligent" brick

LEGOLAND Water Park in Malaysia

Miniland attraction in LEGOLAND California

LEGO master builders with their creations

Artist Nathan Sawaya's LEGO sculpture *Yellow* on display at
The Art of the Brick exhibition in New York, 2013